DATE DUE			

43426

92
AVI

Sommers, Michael A.

Avi

WINFIELD PUBLIC SCHOOL
WINFIELD, IL. 60190

870720 02395   37417B   0001

2/08

Avi

The Library of Author Biographies™

AVI

Michael A. Sommers

The Rosen Publishing Group, Inc., New York

To Vladimir and Oscar

Published in 2004 by The Rosen Publishing Group, Inc.
29 East 21st Street, New York, NY 10010

Library of Congress Cataloging-in-Publication Data

Sommers, Michael A., 1966-
Avi / Michael A. Sommers.— 1st ed.
    p. cm. — (The library of author biographies)
Summary: Discusses the life and work of this popular author, including his writing process and methods, inspirations, a critical discussion of his books, biographical timeline, and awards.
Includes bibliographical references and index.
ISBN 0-8239-4522-7 (library binding)
1. Avi, 1937– —Juvenile literature. 2. Authors, American—20th century—Biography—Juvenile literature. 3. Children's stories—Authorship—Juvenile literature. [1. Avi, 1937– . 2. Authors, American. 3. Authorship.] I. Title. II. Series.
PS3551.V5Z78 2004
813'.54—dc21

                                                              2003009180

Manufactured in the United States of America

Table of Contents

Introduction: They Said He'd Never Be a Writer

Growing up, Avi was constantly told that he would never become a writer. In view of this, the year 2003 began very well for him. On January 27, Avi received the Newbery Medal, the most prestigious award for children's literature in North America. The award-winning novel, *Crispin: The Cross of Lead* (2002), was Avi's fiftieth book for young people.

Crispin, the novel's title character, is a thirteen-year-old peasant boy who lives in a tiny English village. The year is 1377, and Crispin's father, whom he never knew, died in the plague that wiped out a considerable portion of the population of England. At the beginning of the story, Crispin hardly has any identity to speak of. Not only is he fatherless, but he is nameless too—everyone in the village refers to him as "Asta's [his mother's] son." To make matters worse, he can neither read nor write. In fact, he can't do much of anything, aside from, as he gloomily confesses: "[F]ollow an ox. Sow seed. Weed. Gather crops. Thresh wheat and barley."[1]

Then his mother dies, his house is destroyed, and the local steward, who controls the village and all the surrounding land in the name of the powerful Lord Furnival, falsely accuses him of theft and murder. With a reward offered for his head, Crispin must flee in search of liberty. Fortunately, along his journey, he meets up with a red-bearded giant of a man known as Bear. A musician and a juggler, Bear is also a revolutionary who defies authority and the entire medieval English system in which the king, lords, and wealthy church officials dominate the poor, powerless masses.

Under Bear's fierce but kind guidance, Crispin learns how to juggle, play a pipe, snare wild rabbits, and defend himself with a dagger against his enemies. More important, he learns how to ask questions, to challenge authority, and to believe in himself and the freedom to make choices. As Bear tells him: "A wise man—he was a jester by trade—once told me that living by answers is a form of death. It's only questions that keep you living."[2] Crispin's questions lead him to discover his own identity. First, he learns who his real father is. Then he decides who he wants to be.

Unlike Crispin, Avi himself knew early on what he wanted to be: a writer. The only problem was that, at school, he did very poorly in his English classes. Although Avi could read very well, he was a horrible speller. When writing papers, he often used the wrong word or left out words altogether. His papers came back to him completely disfigured by teachers' red pen marks. He even flunked out of one high school because of his terrible grades. Avi's teachers told him that he would never become a writer.

What they didn't know was that he had dysgraphia. Dysgraphic people have trouble writing. They mix up or invert letters and misspell words. For example, Avi might be thinking about "soap," but he will actually write down "soup." An aunt of his once joked that only her nephew could come up with five different ways of spelling a four-letter word. Of course, for Avi this was no laughing matter. He was constantly criticized for what his teachers viewed as sloppiness and a lack of attention.

Fortunately, like the young heroes and heroines of his future novels, Avi challenged the opinions of the adults around him. He was determined to overcome his difficulties and become an author. At the age of twenty-two, he published his first play. At thirty-three, he published his first book of children's stories, *Things That Sometimes Happen: Thirty Very Short Stories for Very Young People* (1970). And at thirty-eight, he published his first novel for young people, *No More Magic* (1975).

The novels that have followed have been exceptionally varied. They range from action-packed adventures and tense, nail-biting thrillers to comic farces, animal stories, and realistic novels about kids in contemporary America. Many are historical novels with settings ranging from Renaissance Italy and nineteenth-century rural Ireland to Colorado in the 1920s. The format and style of Avi's novels also constantly change. Often they are extremely inventive. For example, *City of Light, City of Dark: A Comic Book Novel* (1993) is an illustrated comic book novel set in a futuristic New York City. *Nothing but the Truth*

(1991) is a "documentary novel" constructed out of fictional journal entries, school memos, letters, conversations, newspaper reports, and fragments from a radio talk show.

While critics have been impressed with Avi's mastery of so many different literary styles, Avi views his experimentation with various styles as part of an ongoing search for new and fun ways to tell a story. Avi has one ultimate goal: to create books so exciting that young readers can't put them down. These books are gripping not only because of their fast-paced plots, but because the complex issues force his readers to think.

Like Crispin and like young Avi himself, the characters in Avi's novels are young people who are struggling to navigate in an often confusing and unfair adult world. They are looking for answers, but first they must learn what questions to ask.

1 A Literary Household

Avi (pronounced AH-vee) Wortis and his twin sister, Emily, were born on December 23, 1937, in Manhattan, New York. Avi's father, Joseph, was a psychiatrist, and his mother, Helen, was a social worker. His older brother, Henry, was born in 1935.

Avi is not his real name; it's what a very young Emily called her brother because she was unable to pronounce his name. The rest of the Wortis clan preferred Emily's version, and the name stuck for good. In fact, Avi's original name remains somewhat of a mystery.

When Avi was a year old, the Wortis family moved across the East River to Brooklyn. They lived in an old four-story brownstone house on

Hicks Street, in the historic neighborhood of Brooklyn Heights. The house was built in 1838. Joseph Wortis used one floor as an office where he received his patients. It was in this house that Avi spent his entire childhood until he went away to university.

An Early Reader

Avi's family comes from a long line of writers and storytellers. One of his great-grandfathers had been a professional storyteller/singer at Jewish weddings in the Ukraine (a former republic of the Soviet Union). His job was to entertain wedding guests by telling stories, both sad and funny, about the bride and groom.

Another great-grandfather wrote romance novels about poor Jewish girls who always fell in love with and then married rich gentlemen. Avi also had a grandmother who was a playwright and an aunt who was a journalist. Both of his parents published many works on subjects related to history and the sciences.

When the Wortis children were growing up, relatives were constantly dropping by to visit and tell tales. Their mother also read to them every night. Their house on Hicks Street was filled with books of all kinds. Living in such a bookish atmosphere, it was no wonder that before he even began school, Avi had already taught himself to read. As he recalls:

> When I was five years old—or so the family legend has it—I appeared at the dinner table screaming, "I can read, I can read!" Alas, the legend makes no reference to what it was I read. True or not, that this story was told with pride and amusement suggests how important books were to me—and my family.[1]

Avi devoured adventure stories and mysteries, novels and fairy tales. He read classic and modern literature, not only for children, but for adults as well. He also read, and traded, comic books—but only out on the front porch. His mother considered them so violent that she wouldn't allow them in the house.

When he was quite young, Avi especially enjoyed animal stories. His favorites included Thornton W. Burgess's (1874–1965) tales about Peter Rabbit, Buster Bear, Jerry Muskrat, and Bobby Coon. Later on, he discovered the English classic *The Wind in the Willows* (1908) by Kenneth Grahame, which he read over and over again. Set in the English countryside, the novel tells the adventures of Mole, Ratty, Badger, and Toad—all of whom behave very much like

humans. Although Avi especially loved the boast-
ful, terribly funny Mr. Toad, he identified with
shy and gentle Mole.

In the summertime, while Joseph remained in
the city to work, Helen and the three children
spent time at rented cottages in the countryside
or at the seashore. Later, when Avi was seven, the
Wortises purchased an abandoned farmhouse on
Shelter Island, at the isolated eastern tip of Long
Island, New York. Avi loved the relaxing summers
at Shelter Island. It was a great place to read, and

Books About Beasts

When Avi began writing for young people, he
recalled the animal stories of his childhood. His
first story written for young children was called
Snail Tale: The Adventures of a Rather Small Snail
(1972). It featured not only a snail who read a
book a day, but an adventurer ant and a wise,
advice-giving newt.

His love of animal tales has continued to be
inspirational. In 1995, Avi published *Poppy*,
whose title character is a shy mouse who is
forced to overcome her timidity and battle a
mean old bully of an owl in defense of her home
and her freedom. Set in the fictional Dimwood

continued on next page

---

continued from p. 15

Forest, the book and its main characters, Poppy, her slang-talking mouse boyfriend, Ragweed, and a grumpy porcupine named Ereth, proved so successful that Avi later wrote three sequels: *Poppy and Rye* (1998), *Ragweed* (1999), and *Ereth's Birthday* (2000).

Most recently, Avi published *The Good Dog* (2001). Set in Colorado, this adventure tale revolves around a pet malamute named McKinley who is torn between staying with her master, Jack, and joining a pack of wild wolves. Told from the dog's point of view, Avi hoped the book would satisfy the pet owners he knows who often wonder what their animals are thinking about.

---

its calm, sandy bays were perfect for sailing and swimming. Much later, the island's landscape would inspire the settings for several of Avi's early novels, including *Captain Grey* (1977), *Shadrach's Crossing* (1983; later republished under the title *Smuggler's Island*), and *A Place Called Ugly* (1981).

2 War Games

When Avi began elementary school in the fall of 1942, the United States was in the middle of World War II (1939–1945). American troops were part of the Allied forces fighting for democracy against the Axis powers: Italy, Japan, and Nazi Germany.

The war brought about numerous changes to the Wortises' lives. Joseph Wortis joined the U.S. Navy. As a psychiatrist, he was assigned to New York City, where he counseled marines. Many were traumatized survivors who had experienced, firsthand, the horrors of the battles that took place on the Atlantic Ocean.

Wartime Measures

Meanwhile, severe fighting in the Atlantic caused the U.S. government to worry that Germany might bomb cities along the East Coast, especially New York. As a safety measure, blackouts were often declared. When the blackout siren sounded, people were supposed to stay inside, where their windows were covered with thick black material so that no lights would be seen by enemy bombers. To make sure all lights were out and that nobody was in the streets, some citizens volunteered to patrol the streets. These blackouts made the threat of enemy bombers seem very real to Avi.

As a precautionary measure, Avi and other children had to wear metal identification tags around their necks. In the event of a bombing, children who were lost or had been injured could be identified and reunited with their parents. On Avi's first-grade report card, he received an S (satisfactory) for "Identification Tag," meaning he was never without his tag. Back then, Avi's public school, P.S. 8, awarded first-graders three types of marks: U (unsatisfactory), I (improved), and S (satisfactory). In first grade, almost every mark Avi received was an S. He did receive a U, though, for "Using a Handkerchief" and "Covering Mouth when Coughing." Apparently, he was not very good at either of these things.

During the war, many products were scarce. Natural resources were needed to build airplanes and ships. There was also a great demand for extra food and clothing for American troops overseas. Because of these shortages, many household items, such as sugar, butter, and fabric, were rationed. Other materials, such as metal and paper, were recycled.

There was even a shortage of housing. With so many men and women involved in the war effort, there weren't any workers available to build new homes. Many families who had spare rooms took in boarders. For a time, the Wortises rented out a room in their house. One of their boarders was a medical student who kept a human skeleton in his closet.

Like many other children, Avi contributed to the war effort. After school, he collected scrap metal and old newspapers for recycling. However, despite certain moments of fear and nervousness, life during the war still offered plenty of good times.

School Days

Until eighth grade, Avi's public school was in a residential neighborhood, only a few blocks away from his house. After school, kids got together to play in the street. Although Avi didn't like sports very much—and considered himself pretty bad at them—he did love the Brooklyn Dodgers baseball team. And he rarely missed the chance to listen to a game on the radio.

Even into the late 1940s, very few people in the United States and Canada had television sets. Instead, the two most popular forms of entertainment were radio and movies. When Avi wasn't reading, he often gathered around the radio with Emily and Henry, listening to radio shows. They loved humorous comedians such as Jack Benny and Fred Allen, who were like the David Lettermans of their day. Other favorites were suspenseful adventure tales that featured superheroes Captain Midnight, the Green Hornet, and Ice Man.

Avi waited all week for Saturday mornings to roll around. This was when he and his two best friends, Dickie Macht and Phillip Schwartz, got to spend hours at the local movie theater. A few cartoons were followed by one or two full-length Westerns. The grand finale was an action-adventure film. Its ending left the audience in such a state of nail-biting suspense that the boys would be compelled to return the following Saturday to see how the cliffhanger was resolved.

An Inspiring Past

The events of Avi's childhood—World War II with its shortages and blackouts, street games and radio shows, stories and comic books, Saturdays at the cinema—stimulated his imagination. His experiences allowed him to see the world as a place filled with stories—stories that could be told in many different ways. Later on, these elements of his life would make their way into the books he wrote. For example, nightly radio shows, the war, and even the medical student boarder who kept his skeleton in the closet were all featured in one of Avi's "most autobiographical"[1] novels, *"Who Was That Masked Man, Anyway?"* (1992).

Set in Brooklyn during World War II, the main character, Frankie, is as obsessed with the fictional heroes on radio shows as are many young people today with video games. In fact, Frankie prefers the fictional radio shows to reality. Along with his timid best friend and next-door neighbor, Mario, Frankie acts out his heroic fantasies. These include spying on the "evil" boarder in Frankie's house and setting up a tin-can walkie-talkie system between their houses. The boys also try to arrange a marriage between Frankie's older brother, Tom, who has come home from the war wounded and depressed, and their sixth-grade teacher, Miss Gomez, a movie star look-alike whose boyfriend was killed overseas. (Like Frankie, young Avi loved to playact and make up stories. He did so with his close friend and cousin Michael Saltz, who lived around the corner and who later inspired the character of Mario.)

The imaginative plot of *"Who Was That Masked Man, Anyway?"* is matched by the inventive way it is told. Instead of chapters, the novel is divided into episodes. Each episode alternates between dialogue and actual fragments of 1940s radio scripts. Adventure shows such as *The Green Hornet* and *The Lone Ranger* are reproduced, commercials and all, just as Frankie and Mario would have heard them. The novel's title is a direct quote of the line spoken at the end of *The Lone Ranger* as the masked cowboy hero and his trusty sidekick, Tonto, rode off into the distance.

More recently, both World War II and Avi's Brooklyn childhood served as the backdrop for the novel *Don't You Know There's a War On?* (2001). The format of this novel, which takes place over a seven-day period in March 1943, is more traditional than *"Who Was That Masked Man, Anyway?"* However, the narrative, which recounts each of the seven days, is preceded by real newspaper headlines announcing events that actually happened on each date. Avi's successful integration of historical fact into the narrative highlights the reality of war. The generous sprinkling of quotes from radio programs, war posters, and cinema newsreels adds to the historically authentic feel of the book.

In the novel, eleven-year-old Howie Crispers worries about his father, who is in the U.S. Marines dodging Nazi warships in the North Atlantic. While his mother works long days at the Navy Yard, Howie is responsible for taking care of his pesky little sister, Gloria. When he complains, his mother, like most other characters in the novel, responds by asking him if he's not aware that there's a war going on.

Exceptional times call for exceptional measures. Which is why Howie, as young Avi did, goes around the neighborhood with his best friend, Denny, collecting scrap metal, newspapers, and old clothes for the war effort. He also must stay inside during blackouts, use ration books to buy what little food is in the grocery store, and content himself with the letters his father sends, letters that resemble "Swiss cheese" when they arrive because some parts have been cut out by censors.

Of course, this doesn't stop Howie and Denny from having fun. Aside from listening to the radio adventures of Captain Midnight and Jack Armstrong, the All-American Boy, they go to Saturday afternoon movies. They also mastermind a scheme to save the job of their much-loved sixth-grade teacher at P.S. 8 (Avi's own elementary school), Miss Gossim, whom both boys have desperate crushes on.

Avi confesses that he decided to write this novel after his stepson Jack interviewed him for a school project about life during World War II. As he told Jack, "That interview got me thinking about those times, what my life was like, and how we—as kids—learned to deal with the tensions, shortages, struggles to hold life together in those dark days. For better and for worse we did live differently then."[2]

3 Trouble at School

Avi never liked school very much. He thought that it was mostly boring, and he spent a lot of time daydreaming. Meanwhile, at P.S. 8, Avi's sister, Emily, became friends with a girl named Betty Bao who immigrated from China to the United States in 1947. Bao would later become an author (Betty Bao Lord), and one of her books, *In the Year of the Boar and Jackie Robinson* (1984), features Emily and Avi.

Although Avi's name has been changed to Irvy in Lord's book, Avi admits that Lord's description of him rings quite true. Aside from being shy, he was fascinated with science (in Lord's book, Irvy can't stop talking about spiders) and was very nervous around girls.

Frustration

Because of his dysgraphia (though no one, including Avi, knew that this was his problem at the time), Avi felt like a failure throughout elementary school. The dysgraphia meant that Avi had no control over his writing. If he was writing a paragraph, he might spell a word correctly on the first line, and three lines later, spell the same word incorrectly. For this reason, Avi dreaded Friday, when the class had spelling tests. He also hated getting papers back from his teachers—they were usually filled with big Xs and lots of corrections. The most frustrating part of it all was that even if Avi understood his teachers' corrections, he could not guarantee that he would be able to write the correct word in the future.

Although Avi worked very hard at his writing, his efforts went unnoticed. Unaware of the seriousness of the problem, Avi's teachers simply thought that he wasn't trying hard enough. The constant criticism Avi received made him angry. Unfortunately, it wasn't until he was in his forties that Avi discovered that there was an actual term for his problem. The frustration with his writing was compounded by the fact that Emily was particularly good at spelling and writing. And to make matters worse, throughout elementary school, Avi and Emily were always in the same class. Today, twins are usually assigned to separate classrooms so that one won't be compared with the other.

Unhappy with his situation, at the end of seventh grade, Avi finally rebelled. Instead of being in the same eighth-grade class as Emily, he demanded to be assigned to Mr. Malakoski's class. Mr. Mal, as he was called by the students, was a science teacher and Avi loved science. Not only did he receive high marks in the sciences at school, but at home (like Mario in *"Who Was That Masked Man, Anyway?"*), he often read magazines such as *Popular Science* and *Popular Mechanics*.

Dreams of Flying Machines

Aside from science, Avi had a flair for art. The Wortis family recalls coming downstairs for breakfast one day to discover that nine-year-old Avi had sculpted a nice lump of yellow butter into the shape of a mouse. The only problem with the sculpture was that Avi's dirty hands had turned the butter gray. Avi also liked to draw. Inspired by his science magazines, he took to designing his own airplanes and rockets. For a time, he even considered becoming an aircraft designer.

Apart from designing them, Avi longed to fly the fantastic airplanes he dreamed up. Since that wasn't possible, he did the next best thing—he created fictional characters who were able to fly them. When Avi was around ten years old, he wrote a play set in the twenty-second century, featuring an adventurous pilot named Nick Colt. The original manuscript illustrates his dysgraphia. From one page to the next, the word "scene" is alternately spelled "scean," "scenn," "sean," and "seane."

As an adult, Avi resurrected these childhood fantasies when he wrote the novel *City of Light, City of Dark* (1993). Remembering the adventure comics he read as a boy, Avi teamed up with illustrator Brian Floca and created an original "comic-book novel"—a mixture of narrative, dialogue, and illustrations. Subtitles were provided to translate the Spanish dialogue between main character Carlos Juarez and his mother.

The novel's format and plot were equally imaginative. Set in a futuristic Manhattan, Carlos stumbles upon a magic subway token. Meanwhile, a mysterious parking meter attendant named

Asterel and the villainous Thor Underton—a blind man who makes neon signs—are searching for the token. Carlos meets Sarah Stubbs, the daughter of a candy maker, and together, the teens discover that the token is the secret supply of power in the city. If, by December 21 at noon, the magic token isn't delivered to the dangerous Kurbs, shadowy spirits who rule over the metropolis, the entire city will freeze over.

A final chase scene becomes both suspenseful and fantastic when Carlos and Sarah take to the Manhattan skies on a flying machine that conjures up the imagined planes of Avi's childhood.

An Outsider

It was during elementary school that Avi discovered the joys of the nearby library. As he humorously recalls: "No Friday came without a quick trip to the local library. Why quick? Great selection of books. No public toilet."[1] His favorite books at that time were mostly adventure tales such as Robert Louis Stevenson's *Treasure Island* (1883) and Jules Verne's *20,000 Leagues Under the Sea* (1869). In fact, the first time Avi stayed up all night was because he was so caught up in Jules Verne's novel that he couldn't go to sleep. In the meantime, he also began saving his allowance in order to buy books and create his own library.

Today, Avi claims that he learned much more about how to become a writer from all the books he read at home than from anything he was taught in school. Although he got along well with his family, he often felt somewhat distant from them. In these moments, he often turned to books for company. Avi didn't mind being an outsider. Instead, he found that being alone was "enormously appealing."[2] He relished the chance to hang out by himself and read, write, and daydream.

Avi believed that his parents paid less attention to him than they did to first-born Henry, an excellent student, and to Emily, who had a worrisome heart murmur. He viewed his father as a distant man who never expressed his affections. And Avi still doesn't understand why his highly educated parents never paid attention to his dysgraphia. As an adult he discovered that they had known he had the condition, but they never discussed it with anybody, including Avi himself.

4 "I'm Going to Become a Playwright"

After graduating from P.S. 8 in the spring of 1951, Avi decided to attend Stuyvesant High School in Manhattan. Not only did it have high academic standards with an emphasis on science, but his older brother, Henry, was also enrolled there.

High School

Unfortunately, Stuyvesant proved to be a disastrous choice for Avi. An all-boys school at the time, it was so overcrowded that students went to school in two separate shifts. Among his 5,000 classmates was Walter Dean Myers. Although they never met as students, years later Myers became a celebrated children's author (*Scorpions*, 1988; *Monster*, 1999). With so many students, teachers could give little attention to individual students. During his first semester, Avi failed all of his courses, even wood shop.

As a result, Avi transferred to Elizabeth Irwin High School, a small, coed private school where students received lots of personal attention from teachers. Avi liked this new school a lot better. However, in contrast to Stuyvesant, Elizabeth Irwin's teachers placed a lot of emphasis on writing. This was good news for his classmate, Norma Klein, who went on to become a renowned young adult author (*Mom, the Wolfman and Me*, 1973; *Learning to Fall*, 1989). However, for Avi, writing still proved a torturous experience. No matter how hard he worked, his assignments were still cluttered with errors. By eleventh grade, most of his teachers had given up on him. And Avi had given up on himself.

Then one of his teachers suggested he get special tutoring in writing. The recommended tutor was Ella Ratner, and she lived close to the Wortises. At their first meeting, she asked to see some of Avi's writing, and he showed her one of many plays he had written. After reading it, she turned to him and said, "You're very interesting. You have lots of interesting ideas. If you wrote better people would know that."[1]

Her positive feedback had a great impact on sixteen-year-old Avi. It was the first time someone had encouraged him as a writer. It filled him with hope and determination. From then on, he didn't care about the red marks all over his compositions or his teachers' criticisms. He continued to write his plays. Influenced by the habits of other writers, he also began to keep a journal. In March 1955, he wrote the following into its pages: "I can't wait anymore. I'm going to become a playwright."[2]

The Sporting Life

Never very athletic, in high school Avi had his first, and only, experience with organized team sports when he became captain of the school soccer team. Although the team lost many of its games, Avi nonetheless enjoyed himself. The experience later inspired one of his novels for young people, *S.O.R. Losers* (1984). Reviewed in *The Horn Book Magazine*, an important journal of children's literature, the book was described as "one of the funniest and most original sports sagas [adventures] on record."[3]

In the novel, narrator Ed Sitrow ("Wortis" spelled backwards), his best friend, Pete Saltz (named in honor of Avi's friend and cousin Michael Saltz), and nine other seventh graders have successfully avoided all sports throughout their years at school. However, their accomplishments in writing, art, music, and science are clearly not impressing the adults around them. In the name of the school's "fine sports tradition" and the "American [way of] life,"[4] they are hunted down and made to join the school's soccer team.

Although they do play, the boys refuse to get caught up in the pressure to win placed upon them by the school and parents. Instead, they have the time of their lives—by losing game after game. When told by his teacher that "it's important to win," Ed replies with a puzzled "Why?"[5]

Romeo and Juliet

Later, both Ed Sitrow and Pete Saltz resurface in another novel based on a situation from Avi's own high school years. In *Romeo and Juliet—Together (and Alive!) at Last* (1987), Ed is dumbfounded to discover that his pudgy and poetic pal Pete has a crush on the mousy, bookish Anabell Stackpoole. The only problem is that both are too shy to even look at each other. To help matters, Ed and his friends come up with the idea of staging a school production of Shakespeare's *Romeo and Juliet* and casting Pete and Anabell in the lead roles. The book's hilarious events closely mirror Avi's own experience when he won the lead part in a senior play and developed a major crush on his costar, Alice.

Unfortunately, unlike Anabell and Pete, Alice was unimpressed by Avi's attempts to court her. In fact, during high school, Avi's boyish features and short height, coupled with his shyness, made it difficult for him to impress the numerous girls of his dreams. He was also unhappy to discover that when the girls in his class took a survey of boys to decide who was the cutest, the sexiest, and so on, Avi was chosen as the boy who would make the "best future husband."[6]

He was, however, happier with the comment that accompanied his yearbook photo when he graduated from high school in 1955. The prophetic caption read, "He will be surrounded by books."[6]

Off to College

That same fall, Avi left New York to go to university in Yellow Springs, Ohio. He selected Antioch College, an experimental school where students were given a lot of freedom. Unfortunately, Avi found the lack of structure difficult to cope with. Shortly afterward, he transferred to the more traditional University of Wisconsin in Madison.

At Wisconsin, Avi chose to major in two subjects: history, which had fascinated him since he was a boy, and theater. Although he steered clear of English classes, he was still more determined than ever to become a playwright.

Every year the university had a playwriting contest. In order to ensure fair judging, students submitted their manuscripts anonymously. In Avi's final year of college, he decided to submit a play he had written. When it was handed back to him, it was accompanied by the judge's comments, "This person is obviously not an English-speaking person, but he is making great strides in learning the language and should be encouraged."[7]

Although he graduated in 1959, Avi spent another year at Wisconsin to do graduate work in playwriting. He again submitted a play to the contest. Inspired by his love of American history, he wrote a comedy set around the time of the American Revolution. Entitled *A Little Rebellion*, it ended up winning the contest. The prize included publication in two magazines and a staging of the play at the university's theater. Avi was thrilled. At last he had proved himself as a writer. All that remained to be seen was if he could actually make a living doing what he loved.

5 "Just Say Avi"

fter five years in Wisconsin, Avi was eager to live in a new place. In 1960, he moved to San Francisco, where he had managed to get work as resident playwright for the World Theater. Yet, it was one thing to write plays and quite another to see them produced on the stage. Avi wrote many plays, but the theater was only interested in one of them. And even that one never made it to the stage.

A Struggling Playwright

After a year, Avi became frustrated with the theater scene in San Francisco and decided to try his luck in the theater capital of North

America, New York City. Settling in Manhattan, Avi continued to write. However, he wasn't selling any plays, and he needed to pay the rent. To make money he took any job he could find. He painted signs (complete with spelling mistakes), fried hamburgers, did some carpentry jobs, and worked as an acting coach at a Young Men's Hebrew Association (YMHA) in the Bronx.

At the YMHA, Avi met and fell in love with Joan Gainer, the dance coach. When they began to talk about marriage, Avi began to think about getting a more stable job. One day, wandering around the main New York Public Library building on Fifth Avenue, Avi discovered a job opening for a clerk for the theater collection. It seemed the perfect job for a playwright who loved being surrounded by books.

Soon after he began work, Avi heard some exciting news. In three years, the library's entire performing arts collection would be moving to its own library, part of a new arts complex called Lincoln Center. In order to increase his chances of getting a good job at the new library, Avi decided to pursue a master's degree in library science at Columbia University.

For the next three years, Avi worked during the day and went to school at night. Meanwhile, when time permitted, he continued writing plays—"a trunkful," he admits. "But 99 percent of them weren't any good,"[1] Avi notes.

The First Book

After years of trying unsuccessfully to sell his plays to producers, a friend suggested that Avi try writing a novel. Avi ended up writing two adult novels that he showed to his friend. The friend thought they were good enough to take to a literary agent. As a favor to the friend, the agent tried to sell one of Avi's novels to a publishing house, but the publisher wasn't interested.

In November 1963, Avi and Joan were married. And in 1966, Joan gave birth to the couple's first son, Shaun. Avi was thrilled to be a father, but he worried about how he would support his new family on a librarian's low salary. One way he thought up to earn more money was to make and sell greeting cards. A friend had suggested this after receiving a funny card that Avi had illustrated. Although the scheme never worked out, another friend liked Avi's drawings so much that she asked him to provide illustrations for a children's book she was writing.

When the friend submitted the book to a publishing house, the editor who read it didn't like the story, but she loved the drawings. She called Avi and asked if he would be interested in illustrating books. At first, Avi said no. After all, he was a writer, not an illustrator. However, when the editor promised him that he could not only illustrate but also write a book for her, Avi couldn't refuse.

There was only one problem. In a week, Avi, Joan, and Shaun were leaving the country to spend a year in England. Through an exchange program, Avi was going to work at an English library while an English librarian came to work at his job in New York. How would Avi be able to write and illustrate an entire book in seven days?

Racking his brain for ideas, Avi thought about the bedtime stories he invented for Shaun. Each night he would ask his son what kind of story he wanted to hear, and Shaun would make suggestions such as: "Tell me a story about a glass of water."[2] Avi wrote down a series of these tales and submitted them just as he was about to fly to England.

In the end, the editor who had commissioned the book didn't like the manuscript, but Avi's agent sent the manuscript around until he found a publishing house that was interested in it. As it happened, the editor who accepted Avi's book liked the stories, but didn't think much of the artwork. When *Things That Sometimes Happen*, was finally published in 1970, just the text was by Avi; the illustrations were by another artist.

During the publication of this first book, Avi's agent called him to ask what name he wanted to appear on the book. Avi replied, "Oh, just say Avi."[3] From that time on, that is all he has ever been called by his reading public.

The publication of *Things That Sometimes Happen* was a turning point in Avi's life. First of all, it was the realization of his childhood dream: he had finally proved himself as a writer. Moreover, it revealed to him what kind of writing he should pursue: children's fiction. Suddenly clear about his future, Avi abandoned the third adult novel he had been writing. He also gave up playwriting for good.

When Avi and Joan returned home from England in 1970, they brought with them their recently born son, Kevin. With two children to support, Avi began looking around for a better-paying job. Almost immediately he found one as a librarian at Trenton State College in New Jersey.

That same year, Avi and his family moved to Trenton and life became very busy. Avi was working full-time as a librarian and continued writing new books when he found the time. Some time later, he began teaching children's literature at the college. It was during this time that he began collecting children's books. He often came upon rare first editions of novels at garage sales and secondhand stores. Many times these literary treasures cost only a dime, or even a nickel. Before long, he owned more than 3,000 books!

Avi collected children's books from all periods, but he particularly enjoyed older and historical novels. Later in his career, when he began writing novels for middle school and young adult readers, his book collection was a source of inspiration for the style, language, settings, and descriptive details of his own "historical" tales.

Fatherhood

Avi loved being a father and spending time with Shaun and Kevin. He particularly enjoyed reading to them—both his own books and those of other authors. He claims that he learned more from these reading sessions than his sons did. Through their reaction to various stories, he came to understand how kids react to various books: what they like, what they don't like, how to amuse them and scare them, and how to grab their attention and hold on to it throughout the length of a book.

Perhaps not surprisingly, as Shaun and Kevin grew older, so did the audience Avi wrote for. His first book, *Things That Sometimes Happen*, was a picture book for toddlers, and *Snail Tale* was for young readers. *No More Magic* and subsequent novels were aimed at middle school children. Then in 1981, Avi published *A Place Called Ugly*, his first young adult novel. He remembers quite well how the idea for the story came to him.

> Once upon a time—it was the last day of a Labor Day weekend—I was about to drive my family home. We had been visiting with my parents. My son, Kevin, had been complaining about going back to school. Then, just as we were getting into the car, ready to go, he vanished. My first thought was, "Oh oh, Kevin is hiding so he can stay with his grandparents and miss school." My second thought was, "Hey, that's a good idea for a story."[4]

The novel begins with fourteen-year-old Owen's parents leaving him behind at the end of the summer. Only, unlike Kevin, who only left the car to go the bathroom, Owen refuses to leave his family's "ugly," old, broken-down summer cottage. Threatened by real estate developers who want to bulldoze it to the ground in order to build a luxury hotel, Owen is determined to fight so that things can remain the same.

In this book, Avi tackled one of his favorite themes: a young person who discovers his or her identity by questioning and even fighting adult authority. Following *A Place Called Ugly*, Avi has alternated between writing for middle school and young adult audiences. But the theme of kids challenging adults has remained constant in all of his books.

In 1976, Avi, Joan, and the boys moved from New Jersey to New Hope, Pennsylvania. The family lived there until Avi and Joan separated from each other in 1982. By then, the boys were almost grown. Shaun went off to college, and Avi moved to a house where he could be near Kevin, who lived with Joan.

Soon after Avi and Joan divorced, Avi's sister, Emily, introduced him to a friend of hers from college named Coppélia Kahn. Like Avi, Coppélia was recently divorced. She had a son named Gabriel and taught literature at a college. The two hit it off immediately and before long were making marriage plans. Around this time, Coppélia was offered a job to teach at Brown University, in Providence, Rhode Island. The two decided to move to Providence. However, this time Avi decided he wasn't going to look for a job as a librarian. He was going to try to make a living by writing.

6 Pages Out of History

In Providence, Avi and Coppélia moved into a rambling old historic house. Providence itself dates back to 1636 and has one of the largest concentrations of colonial buildings and landmarks in the United States. Avi was delighted to be surrounded by so much history.

Avi's love of history started in his childhood. He has early memories of his relatives, particularly his grandfather, discussing early American history. The American Revolution especially fascinated him. This interest had led Avi to major in history at the University of Wisconsin. And it wasn't long before it found its way into his novels for young people.

Young Revolutionaries

Captain Grey, Night Journeys (1979), *Encounter at Easton* (1980), and *The Fighting Ground* (1984) take place in the period around the American Revolution. The Revolutionary War against the British monarchy provides a perfect backdrop for these novels in which orphaned American children are forced to rebel against adult rules and authority figures in order to stay alive.

Night Journeys and its sequel, *Encounter at Easton*, were both set in the vicinity of New Hope, Pennsylvania, in the year 1768, just before the Revolutionary War. *Night Journeys* begins when recently orphaned twelve-year-old Peter York is taken in by a Quaker family. When two runaway indentured servants escape, Peter begs his guardian to let him join the search party. He longs to earn the reward offered for their recapture. However, he is conflicted when he discovers that the runaways are children close to his own age. Suddenly, all he can think about is outwitting the adults around him in order to help the children escape. That escape and the continued pursuit of the two runaways is continued in the highly suspenseful *Encounter at Easton*.

One of the two runaways resurfaces years later in *Captain Grey*. Set in 1783, the adolescent hero of *Encounter at Easton* has grown to be a mysterious but brutal pirate—Captain Grey—who kidnaps a recently orphaned eleven-year-old named Kevin. Described by a reviewer in the *New York Times Book Review* as "a robust [rich] pirate adventure with a neat twist,"[1] *Captain Grey* details how Kevin copes with being kidnapped by a lawless group of pirates, all the while trying to free himself and be reunited with his older sister, Cathleen.

Captain Grey is set in the New Jersey wilderness, close to the town of Trenton where Avi had lived and taught and also where *The Fighting Ground* was set. *The Fighting Ground* takes place during the war itself, over an emotionally action-packed twenty-four-hour period in April 1778. When a bell tolls, calling civilians to take up arms against the enemy, thirteen-year-old Jonathan mistakes his father's antiwar stance for cowardice. Dying to fight, he runs off to enlist. However, out on the battlefield, things are far from glamorous. The battle is difficult and bloody, and the corporal Jonathan looked up to reveals himself to be a cruel manipulator. Having discovered that he, himself, is a coward and that war is hell,

Jonathan returns home to his father, alive, but forever changed.

Critics praised this book considerably. Writing in the *Bulletin of the Center for Children's Books*, Zena Sutherland applauded the novel for making "war personal and immediate; not history or event, but experience; near and within oneself, and horrible."[2] As with many of Avi's historical novels, the setting and details are rooted in the past. At the same time, young people can clearly identify with characters whose dilemmas are timeless and universal. Among the numerous awards bestowed upon *The Fighting Ground* was the 1985 Scott O'Dell Award for historical fiction. O'Dell himself, a famous writer of historical fiction for young people, singled Avi out as a talented writer, one who he said was "keep[ing] historical fiction alive"[3] for young people.

Historical Style

As Avi himself confesses, "somewhere along the line, I can't explain where, I developed an understanding of history not as fact but as story."[4] History provides a framework that Avi uses to tell a really good story in a new, challenging way.

For instance, both *Emily Upham's Revenge; or, How Deadwood Dick Saved the Banker's Niece: A Massachusetts Adventure* (1978) and *The History of Helpless Harry: To Which Is Added a Variety of Amusing and Entertaining Adventures* (1980) stemmed from Avi's considerable knowledge of the history of children's literature. Both stories were set in the Victorian period (1875 and 1845, respectively). They were also written in the literary tradition of that era, a period in which books for young readers were often overly sentimental and very moralistic. By imitating and comically exaggerating situations, viewpoints, vocabulary, mannerisms, and even book titles of the mid- to late 1800s, Avi crafted two books that were entertaining while poking fun at social conventions and attitudes (such as sexism and capitalistic greed) that are still in existence today.

Later, in 1996, he returned once again to Victorian literature. The result was *Beyond the Western Sea*, a two-volume epic novel in the spirit of English writer Charles Dickens. One of the world's great novelists, and Avi's all-time favorite authors, Dickens was renowned for novels such as *Oliver Twist* (1838), *Great Expectations* (1859), and *A Tale of Two Cities* (1861). Like Dickens's sweeping novels, *Beyond the Western Sea* featured huge casts of characters and short chapters, each of which ended with a breathtaking cliffhanger. Plots were filled with chance meetings, narrow escapes, and surprising revelations.

Critics mostly praised what one reviewer for *The Horn Book Magazine* called a "rip-roaring rollercoaster ride"[5] about a pair of poor Irish siblings in the 1850s, who, together with the son of their wealthy landlord, run off to Liverpool and board a ship bound for America. Avi himself admits that the fourteen-hour days he put into writing the two-volume novel made it the most difficult book he has written to date.

On Location

For Avi, writing historical fiction consists of more than describing facts and events of the past. Equally important is the choice of a convincing historical setting, or location. When he moves to a new city, Avi always tries to learn everything he can about its history. Actually being in a place allows him to visualize its past and create a believable setting. For example, first New Jersey and then Pennsylvania provided the backdrops for most of his earlier historical novels. And when he settled in Providence, the history of Rhode Island's capital became central to his fiction.

Wondering about the former occupants of the old house where he and his wife were living led Avi to write *Something Upstairs* (1988). The novel begins when a twelve-year-old boy named Kenny moves into an eighteenth-century Providence house (based on Avi's own home) and meets a ghost. Only this particular ghost is a young slave boy named Caleb who was murdered in 1800. As Kenny travels back in time with Caleb to help solve his murder, Avi contrasts Providence of the past with the present-day city. Although Kenny's ability to travel through time adds an element of fantasy to the novel, it also exposes a theme that is important to Avi: History is not dead. Instead, as memory, it is always a living part of the present.

A measure of the success of *Something Upstairs* was that the Providence Preservation Society began including Avi's (and Kenny's) house on its guided historical tours of the city. Other monuments on the tour were featured in another novel of Avi's, *The Man Who Was Poe* (1989).

Written in a style that mimicked the atmospheric mysteries of the real-life writer

Edgar Allan Poe, *The Man Who Was Poe* was described by critic Roger Sutton as a "complex, atmospheric thriller."[6] Set in 1848, the novel begins when young Edmund and his twin sister arrive in Providence from England with their Auntie Pru, in search of their missing mother. When his aunt and then his sister disappear, Edmund has nobody to turn to—except for the cranky, unpredictable, and alcoholic poet, Edgar Allan Poe, whom Avi admired and said was an "incredible and complex figure."[7]

Posing as Auguste Dupin, a fictional detective from the series of Paris mysteries he wrote, Poe agrees to help Edmund unravel the mysteries of his relatives' disappearances. However, his real motivation is to use Edmund's situation as material for a novel he is writing. This creates conflict between the two. Edmund wants nothing more than to be reunited with his family. However, death-obsessed Poe hopes that Edmund's vanished relatives will turn up dead, providing a more interesting ending for his book.

The book's successful mixture of real Providence history and fantasy, of real people (Poe), real fictional characters (Poe's creation, Dupin), and Avi's fictional characters make for a novel that works on many levels. Avi's clever manipulation of these different elements reveals to readers that, at times, the frontiers between real and imagined events are often blurry. Avi also shows that history is as much created as it is factual.

7 Rebels with Causes

In *The Man Who Was Poe*, Edmund's search for his relatives leads him to the port of Providence and to a ship called the *Seahawk*. The same ship became the setting for Avi's next novel, *The True Confessions of Charlotte Doyle* (1990). This book had many similarities to Avi's previous historical novels. Set in 1832, it tells the story of a thirteen-year-old girl from Providence who finds herself alone and forced to survive in a complicated adult world.

The True Confessions of Charlotte Doyle

While Charlotte's well-to-do family isn't dead, they abandon her in England so that she can finish her schooling. Embarking alone—the only child and the only female—on a ship bound for America, the ladylike Charlotte is initially disgusted by the brutish behavior of the crew. When Zachariah, the black cook makes attempts to befriend her, Charlotte, true to the racist conventions of her day, recoils. Instead, she seeks the companionship and protection of authoritarian Captain Jaggery, whose fine clothes and gentlemanly manners remind her of her father.

It isn't long, however, before Charlotte discovers that the crew is justified in planning an uprising against the cruel and vicious captain. Subsequently forced to question the values of her privileged background, Charlotte rebels against everything she was brought up to be. She discards her fancy dresses, chops off her ringlets, and sets to work on the ship. Branded "an unnatural girl"[1] by the captain, she is determined to prove herself as one of the crew. By exhibiting her courage and physical stamina, she ultimately wins over their trust and friendship. In doing so, she discovers her own identity.

In fact, when she finally arrives home in Providence, Charlotte finds that she can no longer be her former self. When her strict father calls her "unnatural,"[2] burns the journal containing her adventures, and confines her to her room, she realizes that, to be true to herself, she has only one option. And so, she returns to the *Seahawk* and the crew that has become her real family.

The novel was praised for its fast-paced plot and its attention to historical detail (including appendices with detailed descriptions of a nineteenth-century ship). But what perhaps registered most with readers and critics alike— the book won many awards including a distinguished Newbery Honor—was the elaboration of one of Avi's most important and ever present themes. In Charlotte's transformation, Avi showed that in order to grow up, children often need to rebel against the adult rules that supposedly protect them, and challenge adult values that may be unjust.

In the acceptance speech he gave when the novel won the *Boston Globe/Horn Book* Award for fiction, Avi began with a humorous tale about a conversation with a film producer who wanted to adapt *The True Confessions of Charlotte Doyle* into a movie. The producer wanted to change one thing about the story—the ending. She felt that Charlotte's leaving home would encourage kids to become runaways. Avi didn't agree, and he told the producer that she had "the wrong Charlotte."[3] Because they couldn't reach an agreement about this matter, the film was never made.

Luckily, other readers had more inspiring reactions to what children's literature professor and critic Catherine Mercier calls the novel's "improbable but deeply satisfying conclusion."[4] In his acceptance speech, Avi talked about some of the comments that had meant the most to him. There was the eleven-year-old boy in a ninja T-shirt who confessed that Charlotte was "going to have a hard time getting married."[5] There was also a woman who told Avi that she finished the book in tears—tears of relief that Charlotte had the courage to follow her own path. Best of all was the eleven-year-old Seattle girl who wrote Avi a letter to say, "Charlotte lives in my heart! Forever!"[6] Said Avi, "If the 'improbable' life I wrote lives in someone's heart as a life possible, then I have already been given the greatest gift a writer can receive."[7]

Nothing but the Truth

The year after publishing *The True Confessions of Charlotte Doyle*, Avi had another great success—and won a second Newbery Honor—with a completely different novel entitled *Nothing but the Truth*. Set in the contemporary United States, the story revolves around ninth-grader Philip Malloy. When poor marks in English keep him off the track team, Philip takes out his resentment on his teacher, Miss Narwin, by humming along loudly during the playing of the "Star-Spangled Banner," which is against school rules.

Although Miss Narwin likes Philip, she sends him to the principal for disrupting class. When he disrupts the class again by loudly singing along with the anthem and refuses to apologize, he is suspended. Furious with Miss Narwin, Philip complains to his parents. Though wrapped up in their own problems, they are nonetheless outraged that their son has been suspended for what they view as patriotism—singing the national anthem. Local school board officials and the media are also horrified. They get wind of Philip's story and repeat various, conflicting versions of it, without any regard for the truth.

And just what is the truth? It is a question that Avi raises again and again in his novels. In

Nothing but the Truth, however, the complicated notion of truth takes center stage. Instead of telling the story from one or even multiple points of view, this realistic "documentary" novel provides the reader with various pieces of evidence. Phone conversations, school memos, letters, and newspaper articles all relate the conflict between Philip and Miss Narwin. It is up to the reader to gather the evidence and judge the truths being told as well as the motives of the tellers. As the title hints, is it really possible to "tell the truth, the whole truth, and nothing but the truth"?

Ultimately, both Philip and Miss Narwin become victims of the so-called truth. As their original conflict becomes blown out of proportion by complete strangers, both become isolated. Abandoned by her colleagues and school authorities, Miss Narwin is forced to leave school. So is Philip, who is misunderstood by his parents, hated by the kids at school, and turned into a poster boy for patriotism by exploitative politicians and complete strangers.

Justice for All

A realistic view of social injustice is yet another major theme that Avi is intensely interested in.

Early on in his life, Avi became aware of the fact that there were many social inequalities in the world. During the 1930s and 1940s, the Wortis family was politically active. They spoke out against racism and supported increased rights for both women and workers. At the time, such views were considered radical, or extreme, by average Americans. As a result, during his youth, Avi was made to feel like an outsider in some social circles.

In many of his books, Avi's youthful heroes and heroines identify injustice and take on the adult authorities and institutions that defend it. For Avi, childhood is a time of innocence, and children often see the adult world with critical eyes. In all of Avi's novels, young people come into contact and conflict with the adult world. For example, Kenny (*Something Upstairs*) takes on racism in the form of slavery, while Charlotte (*The True Confessions of Charlotte Doyle*) battles for the rights of women (like herself) and workers (the brutalized, overworked crew). Ida (*The Secret School*; 2001) fights for children's right to education, while Owen (*A Place Called Ugly*) takes on greedy real estate developers.

In these books, the characters' difficult experiences usually result in the loss of childlike innocence that is an inevitable part of growing up. On the positive side, the tough challenges they face promise to make them braver, smarter, more experienced, and more compassionate adults. Although some might criticize such themes as dangerous because they urge young readers to undermine adult authority, Avi himself sees these challenges to adult authority as an essential part of children's literature. As he stated in an article published by the *The Horn Book Magazine*:

> More than anything else, children's literature is about the place and role of the child in society . . . If we—in the world of children's literature—can help the young stand straight for a moment longer than they would have in the past, help them maintain their ideas and values . . . help them demand—and win— justice, we've added something good to the world.[8]

8 Writing and Rewriting

In 1995, following his separation (and eventual divorce) from Coppélia Kahn, Avi moved to Colorado. He spent six months in Boulder, before moving to Denver, the capital. Although Denver isn't as old as Providence, Avi likes being close to nature and surrounded by mountains and streams. He also enjoys the surprising amount of sunshine there—more than Florida or Southern California, he declares. Together with his new wife, Linda Wright, a publisher, Avi is now part of a "blended family" with five children.

Not surprisingly, local geography and history have already made their way into his most recent novels. *The Good Dog, Perloo the*

Bold (1998), and *The Secret School* all take place against the backdrop of Colorado's mountains.

A Writer's Life

In Colorado, Avi wakes up early and is usually at his computer writing by 8 AM. He often writes for ten or even twelve hours a day, although he usually takes time out to go for a run. Running not only gets Avi out of the house and provides physical activity, but it is also an important part of his writing process. While running, he tries to resolve problems he might be having with the plot of a book.

Avi gets his ideas for novels from many different sources. In fact, Avi has trained himself to see the everyday events around him as stories. Of these stories in his head, only a fraction are actually considered for a possible book. "I can make up a story about anything," says Avi. "That doesn't mean they are all good. But if I have the basis for a story, I can make it good if I choose to."[1]

Sometimes, one event inspires a story. *Wolf Rider* (1985), for example, is based on an anonymous phone call Avi received from a man who claimed to have murdered a woman. Avi kept the man on the phone while the police tried, unsuccessfully, to trace the call. Although the police told Avi that it was probably a crank call, he couldn't follow their advice and forget about it. He found the woman's name in a phone book and called her to tell her she might be in danger. When he later told a journalist this story, the journalist warned Avi not to get involved or the police would end up thinking that he was the caller.

Other times, a combination of events, conversations, memories, and things he has read snowball, over time, into the beginnings of a book. The idea for *Sometimes I Think I Hear My Name* (1982) was triggered by a series of comments Avi overheard. First, there was a remark about the living situation of a teen Avi knew. Then there was a conversation that Avi had with his wife about teens. Then there was a friend's remark about a certain parent and a quotation from a mystery writer that Avi couldn't get out of his head. All of these elements stuck in Avi's brain and inspired him to sit down and begin writing a novel about thirteen-year-old Conrad Murray, who sneaks off to New York to pay surprise visits to the parents who abandoned him.

Once the ideas come, Avi must organize them into a structured story. When he was in school, one of his teachers taught him that the key to writing a play was to start with a written outline of main events. Avi still does this, only now he makes up the outlines in his head instead of writing them out. He considers them the maps that allow him to advance from one part of the story to the next. These story outlines usually change. In fact, Avi often lets the plot events shuffle around in his head for months or even years before he feels ready to begin writing.

In the meantime, he begins researching the story's background. As a former librarian and history lover, this is one part of being a novelist that he really enjoys. Research means not only reading books about other historical periods (the American Revolution, medieval England) or specific subjects (nineteenth-century ships, Edgar Allan Poe), but also looking at photographs, costumes, and illustrations so that he can visualize specific elements.

A Long Process

Once he is finally ready to start writing, he turns on his computer and begins on the first line of the first page. Avi considers the opening of a book crucial. He feels that the first page is where young readers decide whether they want to continue reading or put the book down.

He writes the first sentence, then rewrites it until he is satisfied. He does the same with the first paragraph, the first page, and the first chapter. When he gets to the end of the first chapter, he goes back to rewrite the beginning—not only the chapter, but the entire book!

Working from the beginning, Avi rarely considers the end until he gets to it. As he confesses: "I rewrite the book at this stage maybe forty or fifty times. Over and over again. I have only the vaguest sense of what I'm doing, and I certainly do not have an ending in mind."[2] While writing, Avi often takes notes about characters. Sometimes he creates whole character descriptions, which he keeps beside him, to glance at when he needs to enter into a character's head. As he says, "Often I go through several drafts before I undertake to describe the characters physically—it takes time to get to know them."[3]

Revision Time

Avi usually finishes his entire first draft of a book quite rapidly. He claims that most of his first drafts are so awful he wouldn't even show them to his cat, let alone a human being. Yet a rough draft provides the blueprint for the real work, which is endless writing and rewriting. For this reason, Avi considers himself a very slow worker.

Equally as important as rewriting is rereading. Avi believes you can't be a good writer without first being a good reader. Being an attentive reader allows him to spot problems and make necessary changes to the story.

Having dysgraphia means that Avi can read a passage many times without catching glaring errors. For example, he may write "chess" when he meant "cheese" and only discover this mistake months later. To help focus on errors, Avi often reads text out loud. "Writing is hard for me," he admits. "I love it, but I'm not a natural writer. I don't know who is. I think writing is hard for everyone."[4]

During revisions, Avi counts on the opinions of other readers as well. Particularly important are suggestions made by his agent and his editors. He also seeks feedback from the audience he's writing for—kids. An important part of Avi's career as a writer is the visits he makes to schools and libraries throughout the country. Often he reads manuscripts he is working on. As he says about these visits: "I think it's very important for me to keep these kids in front of my eyes. They're wonderfully interesting and they hold me to the reality of who they are."[5]

How does Avi know when he's finished a book? One of three things usually occurs. Sometimes, he realizes that the changes he's making are so minor—for example, moving a word from one place to another—that they don't make a difference. Other times, his editor calls him up and tells him he has to submit the manuscript he has because it's going to press. And once in a while, Avi decides a book is finished because he simply can't stand looking at it anymore.

In terms of the overall time it takes to write a book, it varies greatly. Avi wrote the first draft of *S.O.R. Losers* in one day. But it took him fourteen years to finish *Bright Shadow* (1985).

Once Avi is content with a final manuscript, it goes to the editor at the publishing house. Even after it has been written and edited, a book may end up not being published. An editor might decide the book isn't good for some reason. Avi might agree or disagree with the editor's decision. If he really believes in the book, he will send it to other publishers, who might accept it.

After Publication

After publication come the reviews. Historically, Avi has a problem with reviewers. He believes that many do not treat children's literature as a serious form of literature. He is also critical of the actual reviews, which generally limit themselves to a paragraph summing up the plot followed by one or two sentences in which the reviewer judges the book as good or bad. Nevertheless, Avi does read reviews of his books, even though negative ones sometimes upset him.

Although Avi doesn't care enormously about awards, he admits that they have been important to his success as a writer. Winning Newbery Honor Books for *The True Confessions of Charlotte Doyle* and *Nothing but the Truth* did a lot for Avi's popularity with readers, teachers, and critics. Before the awards, all of Avi's books had gone out of print. Afterward, all except for his two earliest books were republished in paperback editions. Avi's novels became regulars on teachers' reading lists. Meanwhile, in critics' eyes, Avi came to be considered one of the most important writers of children's literature today, a view reconfirmed by his recent Newbery Medal for *Crispin: The Cross of Lead*.

No matter how many awards he receives, Avi always secretly fears that his next book will be a failure. However, it is this very fear that keeps him striving to make each book the best it can be.

Just as Avi's novels introduce readers to worlds in which young people like themselves fight against the obstacles of an adult world to obtain their goals, Avi's own life story inspires kids that they can do whatever they want in life. After all, Avi proved wrong all the adult critics who said he'd never be a writer. He not only became a writer, but he is an extremely successful one. It is a message that Avi loves to pass on when he visits kids at schools or libraries. In fact, when visiting a school, he often asks to speak to kids with learning disabilities. He describes what happens as the kids enter the room:

> They come in slowly, waiting for yet another pep talk, more instructions. Eyes cast down, they won't even look at me. Their anger glows. I don't say a thing. I lay out pages of my copy-edited manuscripts, which are covered with red marks. "Look here," I say, "see that spelling mistake. There, another spelling mistake. Looks like I forgot to put a capital letter there. Oops! Letter reversal." Their eyes lift. They are listening. And I am among friends.[6]

Interview
with Avi

MICHAEL SOMMERS: Congratulations on your recent Newbery Medal for *Crispin: The Cross of Lead*. What, if any, difference will this make for you as a writer?

AVI: I don't know. What it doesn't do is help me write the next book. What it does do is help bring a lot of my books to more readers. So it has more to do with the past than the future of writing. You want your next book to be better and [an award] gives you the patience to deal with your failure. Writing is hard and it takes a long time.

MICHAEL SOMMERS: In the past you have said that you love writing but find it very difficult. What for you is the most difficult thing about it?

AVI: Writing well. [Laughs.] I think writing well is hard for anybody; it's not unique to me. It's very hard to write something good. But there is enormous satisfaction in getting it to a good place.

MICHAEL SOMMERS: Many of your books are set in the past. Meanwhile, lives of kids today revolve increasingly around CDs, DVDs, computers, and cyberspace. Do you think kids' lives today are even more complicated than when you first started writing in the 1970s?

AVI: I don't think life is so much more complicated today, but there are certainly more pressures placed on young people than when I was growing up. The culture as a whole puts emphasis on more things, and kids feel obligated to conform in the best sense and worst sense.

Families are unfortunately less important in determining values and ways of living. For example, the whole concept of a family sitting down and eating together is simply harder for families to achieve these days. People work more. Both parents work. There's less time. Meanwhile, access to passive media is enormous. I was sitting with my son last night watching a hockey game, and you're just bombarded constantly with "buy this" and "buy that."

MICHAEL SOMMERS: So do you think it's more difficult for twenty-first-century readers to identify with so-called historical novels?

AVI: My job is to make them interesting and engaging. Nobody has any obligation to read anything I write unless it's given to them as a homework assignment. Oh, yes, I think it's more difficult, but not only for young people—for adults, too. Our whole culture is uninterested in history and historical perspective. The culture as a whole doesn't have a good sense of history. Instead, there's tremendous emphasis on the moment now. I read history and I love popular history. Right now I am reading a biography of Queen Elizabeth. It is indeed a wonderful story, though I imagine it could be told in a dull way.

MICHAEL SOMMERS: You tackle a lot of difficult issues in your novels, but even in your non-historical novels you stay clear of many specifically contemporary problems, such as drinking, drugs, AIDS, child abuse, sex . . . Would you like to comment on this?

AVI: Abuse comes up, although it's not referred to as such. Yeah, I don't write about things like drugs and alcohol. Partially because I have no personal experience with these things. Also as a subject about which to write, it doesn't interest me that much. It's just not the way my mind moves along. I think there's a real place for the so-called problem novel. I think it's wonderful for young people to read about and explore [these issues]. It's just not my style. I think I'm somewhat old-fashioned, to tell the truth.

MICHAEL SOMMERS: When you sit down to write a novel, do you have a specific reader in mind, i.e., a boy or girl of a certain age or in a certain grade, shy or outgoing, a slow or enthusiastic reader, a jock or a history buff?

AVI: I tend to focus more on the middle school reader. I know that they respond to a good story. My focus is to write the story as well as I can. I do a lot of school visits and have a fourteen-year-old in my home. One of the reasons I like to do school visits is to have my readers in front of me. That's very important to me. But I don't have any specific reader in mind.

MICHAEL SOMMERS: If you were asked to select one of your novels to be placed in a time capsule that would be opened up in 1,000 years, which novel would you choose and why?

AVI: I have no idea. [Laughs.] I'm working on a new book now and I want it to be the best book I've ever done. I'm excited about it. I'd like to think it will be my best book. Will it be? I don't know. It's just a way of thinking. No, I would not like to pick one book.

MICHAEL SOMMERS: Which of your characters would you most like to sit down and have dinner with? Why?

AVI: [Laughs.] I just don't think of them that way. [Pause.] Oh, a character like Bear from *Crispin*. He seems like an interesting guy who has led a full life. That's an adult character. Maybe a character like Charlotte from *The True Confessions of Charlotte Doyle*. She seems kind of interesting. I don't think of my characters as real that way. Not after I've written them. Well, I might as well say Ereth from *Ereth's Birthday*. He's a porcupine, but he's very funny.

MICHAEL SOMMERS: What's the most memorable thing one of your young readers has said about one of your novels?

AVI: I can remember a couple of things. Just recently a kid who was reading this book *Crispin* said to me "Do people really think this way?"—about the whole medieval worldview. It made me feel like the kid really got into the mind of the character. Then someone said the other day that one of my books was the funniest book she had ever read. I don't know if I believe it, but she said it.

Kids are actually not very articulate about the books they read. They like them or they don't like them. They get very much involved with them, but don't talk about them a great deal. At least not to me.

One girl wrote me about *Beyond the Western Sea*. A character in one of the books gets killed, and she wrote me this furious letter saying that she would never read one of my books again because I had killed her favorite character of all time. I sort of liked that.

Timeline

1937 Avi Wortis is born on December 23, in New York City.
1938 Avi's family moves to Brooklyn.
1942 Avi begins elementary school at P.S. 8.
1951 Avi flunks out his first semester at Stuyvesant High School and transfers to Elizabeth Irwin High School
1955 Avi writes in his journal: "I'm going to become a playwright." He graduates from high school and enters Antioch College in Ohio.
1956 Avi transfers to the University of Wisconsin in Madison and begins a double major in history and playwriting.
1959 Avi graduates from the University of Wisconsin but remains another year to do graduate work in playwriting.

1960 Avi wins the University of Wisconsin's playwriting competition. His play is produced and published in two magazines. He moves to San Francisco and gets a job as resident playwright for the World Theater.

1961 Frustrated with the theater scene in San Francisco, Avi moves to New York City.

1962 Avi begins working as a clerk in the theater collection of the New York Public Library.

1963 Avi marries a dancer named Joan Gainer.

1964 Avi receives a master's degree in library science from Columbia University.

1966 Avi and Joan's first son, Shaun, is born.

1968 Avi and his family spend a year in England, where Avi's second son, Kevin, is born.

1970 Back in the United States, the family moves to Trenton, New Jersey, where Avi takes a job as librarian at Trenton State College. Avi's first book (of short stories) for children, *Things That Sometimes Happen: Thirty Very Short Stories for Very Young People*, is published.

1975 Publication of Avi's first novel for young people, *No More Magic*.

1976 Avi and his family move to New Hope, Pennsylvania.

1982 Avi and Joan are divorced.

1983 Avi marries Coppélia Kahn, a literature

professor, and moves to Providence, Rhode Island. Avi begins writing full-time.

1991 *The True Confessions of Charlotte Doyle* is named a Newbery Honor Book.

1992 *Nothing but the Truth* is named a Newbery Honor Book.

1995 After separating from Coppélia, Avi moves to Colorado—first to Boulder, then to Denver, where he now lives with his third wife, Linda Wright.

2003 *Crispin: The Cross of Lead* is awarded the Newbery Medal.

Selected Reviews from *School Library Journal*

Bright Shadow
October 1985

Gr 5–8—A sensitively written tale which poses philosophical questions about selfishness, selflessness and the terrible burdens of what first appear to be wonderful gifts. Young Morwenna, upon the death of an ancient wizard, finds herself in possession of the world's last five wishes. She soon discovers that this gift is a lonely burden. By a curious trick of fate, a beloved but rather simple and selfish friend believes himself to be in possession of the wishes and constantly gets himself into situations from which Morwenna must extricate him. Freed from his foolishness through his death, Morwenna must live with the knowledge that she could have saved him had she been willing to use her final wish, thus giving up her own life in return. In a straightforward manner, Avi presents a fascinating balance between the simplistic and the complex. The inner conflict constantly taking place within the more mature (though chronologically younger) Morwenna is well contrasted with that of the unsophisticated Swen. A compact and well-told story that should inspire much debate about Morwenna's predicament and what readers would do in her circumstances.

Captain Grey
March 1977

Gr 5–8—Shortly after the American Revolution, young Kevin is captured by pirates, led by Captain Grey, who operate out of a secret cove off the New Jersey coast. From there, they dash out with an armed raft to plunder and sink passing merchant vessels. Kevin's escape plans fail and he is forced by the pirates to become one of their crew. Ultimately, he finds his lost sister and they are rescued by a passing schooner, but Kevin is never able to exact revenge on the elusive Captain Grey who manages to escape. A good, fast-paced adventure, the story is true to the spirit of the times and may catch the attention of slow or reluctant readers, too.

The History of Helpless Harry: To Which Is Added a Variety of Amusing and Entertaining Adventures.
October 1980

Gr 4–6—Horation Stockton Edgeworth is the Harry of the title and his parents, who must be gone for a few days, leave him to the care of the minister's ward, Anne Towbridge. Miss Towbridge arrives with a friend, introduced as John Smith. Harry, who is not fooled, has already stashed away the family money box. Enter Mr. Jeremiah "I'm your friend" Skatch, a flim-flam artist. Also on the scene is Constable Seymour Narbut, a.k.a. the "Great Protector" who thinks Mr. Smith may be a good-for-nothing. Of course, he isn't. Indeed, he's Miss Towbridge's secret husband. By story's end everyone is running in two directions as Harry discovers the awful truth about Jeremiah Skatch and races to save the money box which turns out to have been empty all the time. The year is 1845 and the humor is the old-fashioned let-me-tell-you-a-story type. Subtitled *To Which Is Added a Variety of Amusing and Entertaining Adventures*, it is just that.

A Place Called Ugly
March 1981

Gr 6–9—When fourteen-year-old Owen Coughlin discovers, at summer's end, that the cottage in which he has spent ten happy vacations with his family is threatened by bulldozers so that a resort hotel can be built on the bay site, he refuses—in spite of all entreaties and threats—to return home with his parents. The nondescript, poorly maintained cottage has an aura of beauty for Owen, who has transferred the peace of those vacations to the cottage itself. Then, too, the cottage has been an anchor for Owen as the family moves each time Dad's job demands it. Left alone in the house, Owen faces the anger of the townspeople who see tourist dollars in the new hotel, threats from the town youth who see jobs and a way out of their confining existence and determination equal to his own by the young owner of the property. In a dramatic ending, Owen, having resigned himself to the loss of the cottage, makes himself the instrument of its destruction. The wrenching sadness of lost dreams and times that will not come again is mitigated by Owen's humor, his first love and a fast-paced plot that will keep readers interested. Alternating chapters that intercut fond memories emphasize the bitter-sweetness of this fine book.

S.O.R. Losers
September 1984

Gr 5–7—Avi's latest is a funny spoof on the winning-is-everything syndrome. The special Seventh-Grade Soccer team of South Orange River Middle School is made up of non-athletes par excellence. They are bright students who hate sports in a school that requires every student to play at least one sport. Their coach is a history teacher with no knowledge of soccer and only a bit more enthusiasm for winning than his team. When they lose their first games by enormous margins, they're surprised to learn that the school and their parents are very upset. Ed Sitrow, the team captain who tells the story, even sees his blossoming romance die in the bud. But the team, undaunted, is determined to play no better than they know how to. As one player puts it, " . . . if we just go on out there, relax, and do our best, and not worry so much, we'll lose." It all comes out for the worst, or rather the better, in the end. A delightful story, and an easy read for sports fans.

Shadrach's Crossing
May 1983

Gr 5–8—Once again, Avi makes use of an historical backdrop for a fast-moving plot involving a heroic young person. It is 1932: time of the Great Depression and Prohibition. Shadrach Faherty, disgusted by the passivity of his family and neighbors, decides to take on single-handedly a group of liquor smugglers who are terrorizing his poor island home. His attempts to discover the identities and foil the plans of the smuggler produce some gripping scenes and provide the narrative with most of its substance. A sense of oppressive poverty and impotent anger—paralyzing the community and forcing Shad's father to admit his helplessness to his son—is sustained throughout. Readers might be puzzled by the author's portrayal of the Coast Guard, who seems rather timid and unknowledgeable in the ways of catching smugglers red-handed: Shad, with his shrewdness and stubborn courage, outshines them by far. This exciting story will appeal to a wide range of ages and abilities, particularly to those who shy away from heavier historical fiction.

List of
Selected Works

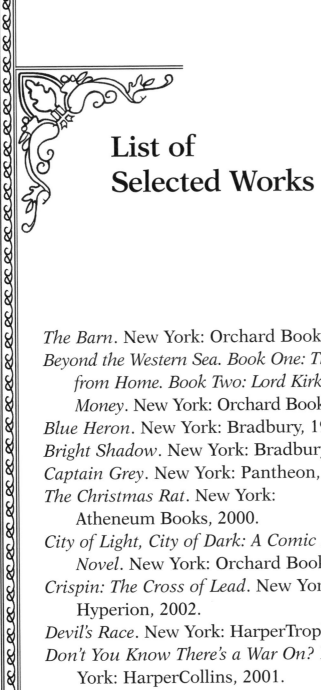

The Barn. New York: Orchard Books, 1994.
Beyond the Western Sea. Book One: The Escape from Home. Book Two: Lord Kirkle's Money. New York: Orchard Books, 1996.
Blue Heron. New York: Bradbury, 1992.
Bright Shadow. New York: Bradbury, 1985.
Captain Grey. New York: Pantheon, 1977.
The Christmas Rat. New York: Atheneum Books, 2000.
City of Light, City of Dark: A Comic Book Novel. New York: Orchard Books, 1993.
Crispin: The Cross of Lead. New York: Hyperion, 2002.
Devil's Race. New York: HarperTrophy, 1984.
Don't You Know There's a War On? New York: HarperCollins, 2001.

Emily Upham's Revenge; or, How Deadwood Dick Saved the Banker's Niece: A Massachusetts Adventure. New York: Pantheon, 1978.

Encounter at Easton. New York: Pantheon, 1980.

Ereth's Birthday. New York: HarperCollins, 2000.

The Fighting Ground. New York: Lippincott, 1984.

The Good Dog. New York: Atheneum Books for Young Readers, 2001.

The History of Helpless Harry: To Which Is Added a Variety of Amusing and Entertaining Adventures. New York: Pantheon, 1980.

Man from the Sky. New York: Knopf, 1980.

The Man Who Was Poe. New York: Orchard Books, 1989.

Midnight Magic. New York: Scholastic, 1999.

Night Journeys. New York: Pantheon, 1979.

No More Magic. New York: Pantheon, 1975.

Nothing but the Truth. New York: Orchard Books, 1991.

Perloo the Bold. New York: Scholastic, 1999.

A Place Called Ugly. New York: Pantheon, 1981.

Poppy. New York: Orchard Books, 1995.

Poppy and Rye. New York: Avon Books, 1998.

Punch with Judy. New York: Bradbury, 1993.

Ragweed. New York: Avon Books, 1999.

Romeo and Juliet—Together (And Alive!) at Last. New York: Orchard Books, 1987.

The Secret School. New York: Harcourt, 2001.

Shadrach's Crossing. New York: Pantheon, 1983.

Snail Tale: The Adventures of a Rather Small Snail. New York: Pantheon, 1972.

Something Upstairs. New York: Orchard Books, 1988.

Sometimes I Think I Hear My Name. New York: Pantheon, 1982.

S.O.R. Losers. New York: Bradbury, 1984.

Things That Sometimes Happen: Thirty Very Short Stories for Very Young People. New York: Atheneum Books for Young Readers, 2002.

The True Confessions of Charlotte Doyle. New York: Orchard Books, 1990.

Who Stole the Wizard of Oz? New York: Knopf, 1981.

"Who Was That Masked Man, Anyway?" New York: Orchard Books, 1992.

Windcatcher. New York: Bradbury, 1991.

Wolf Rider. New York: Bradbury, 1986.

List of Selected Awards

***Beyond the Western Sea* (1996)**
Booklist, Editor's Choice (1996)

***Blue Heron* (1992)**
American Library Association, Best Books
for Young Adult List (1993)

***City of Light, City of Dark* (1993)**
Publishers Weekly, Best Children's Books of
the Year (1993)

***Crispin: The Cross of Lead* (2002)**
Newbery Medal (2003)

***The Fighting Ground* (1984)**
American Library Association, Notable
Book (1984)
American Library Association, Best Books
for Young Adults (1984)
Scott O'Dell Award, Best Historical
Fiction (1984)

Man From the Sky (1980)
International Reading Association, Children's
   Choice (1980)

The Man Who Was Poe (1989)
Library of Congress, Best Books of the
   Year (1990)

Night Journeys (1979)
School Library Journal, Best Books of the
   Year (1980)

No More Magic (1975)
Mystery Writers of America, Special Award (1975)

Nothing but the Truth (1991)
American Booksellers Children's Choice
   List (1992)
American Library Association, Notable
   Book (1992)
American Library Association, Young Adult
   Services Division, Best Books for Young
   Adults (1992)
Booklist, Editor's Choice (1992)
Boston Globe/Horn Book Honor Book (1992)
Bulletin of the Center for Children's Books, Blue
   Ribbon Book (1992)
Publishers Weekly, Best Books (1991)
Horn Book Fanfare (1992)

Library of Congress, Best Books for
  Children (1992)
Newbery Honor Book (1992)

Poppy **(1995)**
Booklist Editor's Choice (1995)
Boston Globe/Horn Book Award (1995)

Romeo and Juliet—Together (and Alive!) at Last **(1987)**
American Library Association Young Adult
  Services Division, Recommended Book for
  Reluctant Readers (1988)
International Reading Association, Children's
  Choice (1988)

Shadrach's Crossing **(1983)**
Mystery Writers of America, Special Award (1983)

Something Upstairs **(1988)**
Library of Congress, Best Books of the Year
  (1989)

The True Confessions of Charlotte Doyle **(1990)**
American Library Association, Notable
  Book (1990)
American Library Association's Young Adult
  Services Division (1991)
Booklist Editor's Choice (1990)
Boston Globe/Horn Book Award (1991)

Horn Book Fanfare (1992)

International Reading Association, Children's Choice (1990)

Library of Congress, 100 Best Books for Children (1991)

Newbery Honor Book (1991)

School Library Journal, Best Books of 1990

"Who Was That Masked Man, Anyway?" **(1992)**

American Booksellers Pick of the List (1993)

American Library Association, Notable Book (1993)

Booklist Editors' Choice (1992)

School Library Journal Best Book (1992)

Wolf Rider **(1986)**

American Library Association, Best Books for Young Adults (1986)

American Library Association, Young Adult Services Division, Recommended Book for Reluctant Readers (1986)

American Library Association, Young Adult Services Division, Mystery Genre Book List (1986)

Booklist, Best Book of the Eighties (1986)

Glossary

blackout When all lights are turned off or hidden, making it difficult for enemy aircraft to drop bombs on targets.

brownstone A house built with reddish-brown colored stones.

capitalism An economic system that favors business transactions that are uncontrolled by government interference.

compassionate Sympathetic.

conventions Standard rules of conduct or behavior.

dysgraphia A writing disability that leads to misspelling of words and inversion of letters.

epic An artwork, such as a novel or poem, of grand, heroic size and subject matter.

exploitative Using someone else for selfish reasons.

farce A light dramatic play or novel with much comedy and an improbable plot.

hypocritical Characterized by saying something while believing or practicing something else.

indentured servant A servant who is bound to a master by contract.

jester A merrymaker or jokester who made his living entertaining people (usually in the Middle Ages).

malamute A breed of Alaskan dog used to pull sleds.

monarchy A system of government in which one person, usually a king or queen, rules the country.

newsreel A short film of recent news clips.

plague A highly contagious disease that killed many Europeans during the Middle Ages.

Poe, Edgar Allan Famous American writer and poet (1809–1849) renowned for mysteries and tales of the supernatural.

prestigious Distinguished, highly regarded.

prophetic Being able to predict the future.

Quaker A member of a sect of Christianity known as the Religious Society of Friends that formed in seventeenth-century England. Many of its members settled in the colonies in New England.

ration To cut down or limit one's use of a product that is scarce.

recoil To shrink or spring back in fear or disgust.

snare A trapping device used to capture birds and small mammals.

steward A person in charge of another's house, property, or affairs.

thresh To beat the stems or husks of grain or cereal plants in order to separate the seeds.

traumatized Psychologically hurt or damaged.

undermine To sabotage or weaken.

Victorian Relating to the reign of England's Queen Victoria (1837–1901).

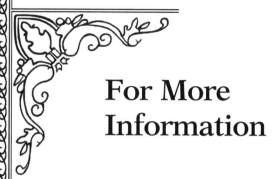

For More Information

Web Sites

Due to the changing nature of Internet links, The Rosen Publishing Group, Inc., has developed on online list of Web sites related to the subject of this book. This site is updated regularly. Please use this link to access the list:

http://www.rosenlinks.com/lab/avi

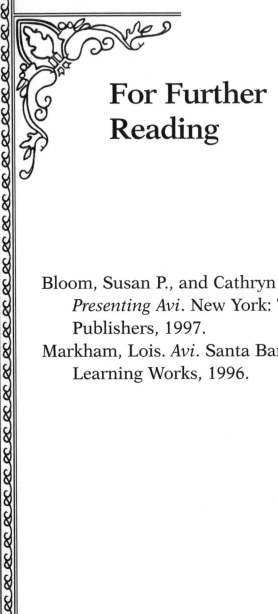

For Further Reading

Bloom, Susan P., and Cathryn M. Mercier. *Presenting Avi*. New York: Twayne Publishers, 1997.

Markham, Lois. *Avi*. Santa Barbara, CA: Learning Works, 1996.

Bibliography

Avi: The Official Web Site. Retrieved January 2003 (http://www.avi-writer.com).

Avi. Acceptance speech for the *Boston Globe/Horn Book* Fiction Award for *The True Confessions of Charlotte Doyle*. The *Horn Book Magazine*, January/February 1992, pp. 24–27.

Avi. "All That Glitters." *The Horn Book Magazine*, September/October 1987, pp. 569–576.

Avi. *Blue Heron*. New York: Bradbury, 1992.

Avi. *Bright Shadow*. New York: Bradbury, 1985.

Avi. "The Child in Children's Literature." *The Horn Book Magazine*, January/February 1993, pp. 40–50.

Avi. *City of Light, City of Dark: A Comic Book*

Novel. New York: Orchard Books, 1993.

Avi. *Crispin: The Cross of Lead*. New York: Hyperion, 2002.

Avi. *Devil's Race*. New York: HarperTrophy, 1984.

Avi. *Don't You Know There's a War On?* New York: HarperCollins, 2001.

Avi. *Encounter at Easton*. New York: Morrow Junior Books, 1994.

Avi. "Future Classics." *The Horn Book Magazine*, November/December 2000, p. 647.

Avi. "I Can Read, I Can Read!" *The Horn Book Magazine*, March/April 1994, pp. 166–169.

Avi. *The Man Who Was Poe*. New York: Avon Flare, 1991.

Avi. *Night Journeys*. New York: Morrow Junior Books, 1994.

Avi. *Nothing but the Truth*. New York: Avon Flare, 1993.

Avi. "Reviewing the Reviewers." *School Library Journal*, March 1986, pp. 114–115.

Avi. *Romeo and Juliet—Together (And Alive!) at Last*. New York: Avon Camelot, 1988.

Avi and Betty Miles. "School Visits: The Author's Viewpoint." *School Library Journal*, January 1987, pp. 21–26.

Avi. *The Secret School*. New York: Harcourt, 2001.

Avi. *Sometimes I Think I Hear My Name.* New York: Avon Flare, 1995.

Avi. *S.O.R. Losers.* New York: Simon & Schuster, 1984.

Avi. *The True Confessions of Charlotte Doyle.* New York: Orchard Books, 1990.

Avi. *"Who Was That Masked Man, Anyway?"* New York: Orchard Books, 1992.

Avi. *Wolf Rider.* New York: Aladdin, 1993.

Benson, Sonia. *Something About the Author.* Vol. 71. Diane Teligen, ed. Detroit: Gale Group, 1993.

Bloom, Susan P., and Cathryn M. Mercier. *Presenting Avi.* New York: Twayne Publishers, 1997.

Burns, Mary M. "Review of *S.O.R. Losers.*" *The Horn Book Magazine.* January 1985, p. 49.

Educational Paperback Association Web Site. Author Biographies: Avi. Retrieved January 2003 (http://www.edupaperback.org/authorbios/avi.html).

Jackson, Richard. "We." *The Horn Book Magazine,* May/June 1993, pp. 296–302.

Jaffee, Cyrisse. "Review of *Emily Upham's Revenge.*" *School Library Journal,* March 1978, p. 124.

Jones, Trev. "Review *of The True Confessions of*

Charlotte Doyle." School Library Journal,
September 1990, p. 221.
KidSpace@the Internet Public Library. The
Author Page: Avi. Retrieved January 2003
(http://www.ipl.org/div/kidspace/askauthor/
Avi.html).
KidsReads.com. Avi Interview. Retrieved
January 2003 (http://www.kidsreads.com/
authors/au-avi.asp).
Marinak, Barbara Ann. "Interview with Avi."
Book Report, March/April 1992, p. 26.
Markham Lois. *Avi*. Santa Barbara, CA: The
Learning Works, 1996.
Mercier, Catherine M. "Review of *The True
Confessions of Charlotte Doyle." The Five
Owls*, January/February 1991, p. 57.
O'Connor, Jane. "Review of *Captain Grey." New
York Times Book Review*, September 11,
1977, p. 30.
"Review of *Beyond the Western Sea." The Horn
Book Magazine*, July/August 1996, p. 461.
Scholastic Books. "About the Author. Avi's
Biography." Retrieved January 2003
(http://www2.scholastic.com/teachers/
authorsandbooks).
Scholastic Books. Avi's Interview Transcript.
Retrieved January 2003

(http://www2.scholastic.com/teachers/
authorsandbooks).

Senick, Gerald J., ed. *Children's Literature
Review*. Vol. 24. Detroit, MI: Gale
Group, 1991.

SimonSaysKids.com. "Authors and Illustrators:
Avi." Retrieved February 2003
(http://www.simonsays.com/subs/pdfs/
kids/Avi.pdf).

Stan, Susan. "Conversations: Avi." *The Five
Owls*, January/February 1990, p. 45.

Sutherland, Zena. "Review of *The Fighting
Ground*." *Bulletin of the Center for Children's
Books*, June 1984, p. 180.

Sutton, Roger. "Review of *The Man Who Was
Poe*." *Bulletin of the Center for Children's
Books*, October 1989, p. 27.

Source Notes

Introduction
1. Avi, *Crispin: The Cross of Lead* (New York: Hyperion, 2002), p. 77.
2. Ibid., pp. 97–98.

Chapter 1
1. Avi, "I Can Read, I Can Read!" *The Horn Book Magazine*, March/April 1994, p. 166.

Chapter 2
1. Lois Markham, *Avi* (Santa Barbara, CA: The Learning Works, 1996), p. 16.
2. Avi-Writer.com, "About Avi's Books." Retrieved February 2003 (http://www.avi-writer.com).

Chapter 3
1. Avi, "I Can Read, I Can Read!" *The Horn Book*

Magazine, March/April 1994, p. 166.
2. Lois Markham, *Avi* (Santa Barbara, CA: The Learning Works, 1996), p. 41.

Chapter 4

1. Lois Markham, *Avi* (Santa Barbara, CA: The Learning Works, 1996), p. 48.
2. Ibid.
3. Mary M. Burns, "Review of *S.O.R. Losers*," *The Horn Book Magazine*, January 1985, p. 49.
4. Avi, *S.O.R. Losers* (New York: Simon & Schuster, 1984), p. 71.
5. Markham, p. 49.
6. Ibid., p. 50.
7. Ibid., p. 51.

Chapter 5

1. Lois Markham, *Avi* (Santa Barbara, CA: The Learning Works, 1996), p. 56.
2. Ibid., pp. 57–58.
3. Ibid., p. 59.
4. Avi-Writer.com, "*A Place Called Ugly.*" Retrieved February 2003 (http://www.avi-writer.com).

Chapter 6

1. Jane O'Connor, "Review of *Captain Grey*," *New York Times Book Review*, September 11, 1977, p. 30.
2. Zena Sutherland, "Review of *The Fighting Ground*," *Bulletin of the Center for Children's Books*, June 1984, p. 180.

3. Barbara Ann Marinak, "Interview with Avi," *Book Report*, March/April 1992, p. 26.

4. Sonia Benson, *Something About the Author*, Vol. 71 (Detroit, MI: Gale Group, 1993), p. 11.

5. "Review of *Beyond the Western Sea*," *The Horn Book Magazine*, July/August 1996, p. 461.

6. Roger Sutton, "Review of *The Man Who Was Poe*," *Bulletin of the Center for Children's Books*, October 1989, p. 27.

7. Susan Stan, "Interview with Avi," *The Five Owls*, January/February 1990, p. 45.

Chapter 7

1. Avi, *The True Confessions of Charlotte Doyle* (New York: Orchard Books, 1990), p. 169.

2. Ibid., p. 207.

3. Avi, *"The True Confessions of Charlotte Doyle,"* *The Horn Book Magazine*, January/February 1992, p. 25.

4. Catherine M. Mercier, "Review of *The True Confessions of Charlotte Doyle*," *The Five Owls*, January/February 1991, p. 57.

5. Avi, *"The True Confessions of Charlotte Doyle,"* *The Horn Book Magazine*, p. 25.

6. Ibid., p. 26.

7. Ibid., p. 27.

8. Avi, *"All That Glitters,"* *The Horn Book Magazine*, September/October 1987, p. 576.

Chapter 8

1. Lois Markham, *Avi* (Santa Barbara, CA: The Learning Works, 1996), p. 82.
2. Susan P. Bloom and Catherine M. Mercier, *Presenting Avi* (New York: Twayne Publishers, 1997), p. 152.
3. *Avi*, from Pantheon Books Library Market Press Release, no date.
4. Bloom and Mercier, p. 150.
5. Sonia Benson, *Something About the Author*, Vol. 71 (Detroit: Gale Group, 1993), p. 14.
6. Avi and Betty Miles, "School Visits: The Author's Viewpoint," *School Library Journal*, January 1987, p. 21.

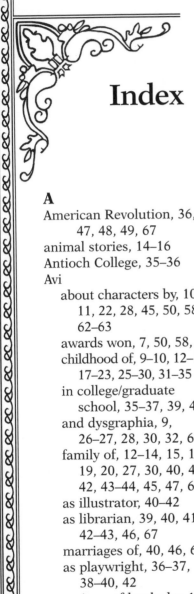

Index

About the Author

Michael A. Sommers is a freelance writer.

Photo Credits

Cover image © Gary Isaacs, Interior © Lorie K. Stover.

Designer: Tahara Hasan; Editor: Annie Sommers